RETAIL SUCCESS:
MASTER THE ART OF SELLING ANYTHING IN LESS THAN 1 HOUR !

Author: Petratou Anastasia
Editor: Jessica Fentiman

Table of Contents

Introduction

In the 21st century great selling skills are without a doubt, a must-have for anyone. As you may have already realized, every job position includes a "sales" aspect. It doesn't matter if you are selling products, services, or even yourself (e.g. at an interview or dare I say, to a prospective date) it all comes down to the same thing. Your goal is to get other people to accept you, your product, or your idea. This concise book is written in an easy-to-understand language, and will give you a summary of how sales work (with examples from multiple industries). It is meant for you to read in under one hour and be able to hone the skill of selling anything to anyone. Because sales CAN be taught. There is no hype or theoretical practices, just proven and effective "how-to" strategies to help you increase your sales volume immediately. Simply follow the steps, practice them, and watch your sales double, even triple, over time!

Chapter 1.
Knowing Your Audience

The first step in selling any product or service, is to know **who** you are selling to! Once you manage to identify your customers, you will then be able to discover the best approach in selling to them. Just like I know you (my audience), do not care about a lengthy introduction with definitions of what sales mean. You are educated enough to know the basics and want results fast, with clear guidelines: *If I do 1,2,3 = I get the result I want.* So, let's jump straight into it.

Before we even start discussing sales techniques and practices, you need to figure out who your selling audience is. You need to be aware of the characteristics that the majority of your customers have in common if you want to increase your chances of selling. This includes knowing the demographics of your typical consumer. Simply put, what is your target group?

As you know, one shoe does not fit all, therefore, your target group cannot be everyone. There is no "one" product that can be successfully marketed to the entire population, as different groups of people have different needs and wants. Keep in mind, that in certain cases, not all of your products necessarily share the same target group. For example, you could be selling men's, women's, and children's clothing, so your approach to selling should be different depending on the customer in front of you. If you haven't given any thought to what your target group is, now is the best time to figure it out!

In order to understand what your target group is, you should be able to answer the following questions (on average):

1. What age are your customers?
2. Which gender do you sell to most?
3. What is their nationality?
4. What is their level of education?
5. What is their income? (I don't mean the exact number, just a ballpark. Is their income high or low?)
6. What line of work are they in?
7. What is their relationship status? (single or married, not if "*it is complicated*", we'll leave that to Facebook)
8. What are their interests and lifestyle like?

Every single one of these questions will bring you closer to selling the right product to the right consumer and figure out faster and more efficient ways to up-sell & cross-sell. For instance, you may have noticed that a product is performing best for ages over 40. Therefore, whenever a customer in that age group walks into your store, you already know what they are most likely going to buy, and in turn what product you should be showing to them first. Or, if we stick to the first example, (in which you are selling men's, women's, and children's clothing) let's say you are assisting a female customer purchasing a dress for herself, who you find out is married with two children. This is your opportunity to propose (and up-sell) additional items for her spouse and children. The more information you are able to gather regarding your customer, the easier it will be for you to sell to them.

Chapter 2.
Knowing Your Product

The second step in successfully selling any product or service is knowing everything there is to know about your product by heart. The more you know about your product, the more confident you will be in selling it. To know your product well, you need to be aware of every positive and negative trait it possesses, as well as all its features. This will assist you in better communicating how the customer will benefit from your product or service. After all, consumers will only purchase products if they get some kind of benefit out of them. Some features and aspects of physical products that you can use to your advantage and that you should be aware of (apart from their positive and negative qualities) include:

1. **Sizing**
2. **Stock Availability**
3. **Color**
4. **Price Range**
5. **Use**
6. **Fabrics**
7. **Technical construction**
8. **Durability and product life expectancy**
9. **Knowledge of similar competitor products**
10. **Company information**

1. Sizing

If you are in the fashion industry you should know everything there is to know about sizes. That entails what size each article comes in, keeping in mind that not all items in a store are available in every size, and in-store availability of that item may vary. Furthermore, you need to know the size-weight/height equivalent. This means for example, your size Small in t-shirts is suitable for people up to 50kg with a maximum height of 170cm. You should also be aware if your sizes run equal to, smaller, or bigger than industry standards. Another attribute you should be aware of regarding sizes, is which clothing lines, suit which body type. "A"-line dresses are perfect for women with a wider hip line for instance, and longer dresses are ideal for taller women. Finally, should you be working with customers not residing in your country (i.e. Tourists), it would be helpful to know the different sizing metrics around the world. For example, a European size Small is equivalent to a UK size 8.

2. Stock Availability

Stock availability knowledge is based on:

A.) Being familiar with what stock you have available in the products displayed inside your store and,

B.) what stock you have available in your warehouse.

This will prove helpful if a customer is looking for something that cannot be found in the sales area, but you remember that you have what they want stored in your warehouse. As you probably already know, products are withdrawn from the store after a certain time period, in order to give space to new arrivals or to refresh the visual merchandising. So, it would benefit you if you could remember which products were removed from the sales area.

3. Color

I can already hear all the men reading this part thinking *"What is it with women and color? Do we really need to find out if the customer's favorite color is blue??"* The answer is Yes. You do. That is if you really want to increase your chances of selling. People associate colors with different things. That doesn't necessarily mean discovering their favorite color per se, it just means finding out what product color they are interested in buying. One customer might prefer a black PC, and another might only be interested in a pink one. Needless to say, you should know all of your products' color variants. You should also try to discover the reason behind your clients requesting a specific color. For example, a customer might say that he or she is only interested in purchasing black shoes <u>because</u> it is a color that "goes with everything". Aha! In this case you can then argue that brown is also a neutral color that can be paired easily with anything, which gives you a larger option range for them to choose from. **Remember, the more options you present a consumer, the more likely they are to find something to purchase**.

4. Price Range

Knowing your price range does not mean knowing each single product price by heart (although it would be great if you managed to learn that too), it means being able to answer the question *"How much do your products cost?"*. Therefore, you should know the price range of each product category you have to offer. For example, your e-courses start at 10,99$ and go up to 50,99$, or your jeans start at 60$ and go up to 150$. Providing the customer with that price-range knowledge, will assist you in finding the optimal product suitable for their budget requirements.

5. Use

Use is just as important. Knowing when and how the customer is planning to use your product will help you sell the ideal product or service. For instance, if a customer mentions that they are looking for a black suit to wear to work, you can provide more options that match the description of "appropriate work attire". Or if a consumer is interested in buying a vacation to Italy because of the warm weather and beaches, you can propose more alternatives with the same features, such as Greece or Thailand.

6. Fabrics

If you are in the fashion industry it would be a good idea to know everything with respect to the fabrics used in your products' construction. For example, if you are selling a cotton pajama you will be able to highlight the properties of cotton (which are: it is breathable, light to wear and hypo-allergic). However, it would be optimal if you also knew the negative traits of each fabric in order to be prepared for any objections made by consumers. For instance, if a customer says that they are only interested in cotton products (this significantly reduces the options you can provide them) because they are breathable, you could argue that cotton also wrinkles easily. In this example you could then show them a viscose garment you have in stock, as it is both breathable and doesn't wrinkle. Most products, such as clothes, bags, and sometimes shoes, feature a tag with the synthesis of the product. My advice is to go over those tags and learn which fabrics are used in each garment, as well as studying the properties of each fabric (e.g. durability, heat retention, washing, and ironing demands etc).

7. Technical construction

Even if you are not in the clothing industry and fabrics do not apply to your product category, it is still important to know the construction of your products; you should know what materials were used in the manufacturing of your product. What are the strengths of these materials? Are they more durable than other similar materials? For example, if you are selling cars, you should know why one car engine is better than another. What about its construction makes it unique or higher quality? In the beginning of this chapter I also mentioned being familiar with the negative properties of your product or service. This probably appears bizarre to you; however, you need to know what objections you could face from your customers, in order to be prepared to argue your way out of them.

E.g. A customer that is interested in buying a certain cell phone, says that the video quality of that particular phone is not good. If you anticipated that objection, you will have an answer prepared. That could be highlighting other positive traits the phone has (large storage space, easy navigation etc.), or explaining to the customer they can find higher video quality on other, more expensive, devices you offer.

8. Durability and product life expectancy

Durability and product life expectancy is also essential for you to be familiar with. It can even be your top selling point. For instance, if you are selling a washing machine that you know has a life expectancy of 10 years, you can explain to the customer that this washing machine is their best option, because they will benefit from its longevity and therefore will not have to invest in a new washing machine any time soon.

9. Knowledge of similar competitor products

Having knowledge of similar products your competitors are offering is imperative to selling, because you need to be able to answer the following questions: Why should the customer prefer you over your competitor? What makes your products better or differentiates them from your competitors? It could be your product price, design, or quality, for example, or even the level of assistance you offer to your clients versus your competitor. However, in order to identify the ways your products are different from the ones your competitors are offering, you need to do your research first. So, visit your competitors store or website and investigate their products and offers. You might even pick up on a tip or two (For the record, I am not suggesting copying or stealing ideas from your competitors, but it will serve you to learn from people who have better practices in place than you). There is always room for improvement, so you should consistently strive to learn from the best.

10. Company information

Company information knowledge might not appear as a product trait at first glance; however it can be, since people associate products with the brand behind them. As you may have noticed, clients are more likely to purchase from a brand they know, trust, and value. Therefore, you should be able to communicate relevant information about your company, such as: where your products are manufactured, how often you have new deliveries, when your company was established (hence how many years of experience your brand has under its belt), and what your company values are. These topics can aid you in getting the customer to trust you and your company, which in turn will lead to more sales.

Chapter 3.
The Three Big Secrets of Every Great Salesperson

So far, we have covered obtaining knowledge regarding your audience and your products. It's time to talk about YOU. You may have acquired all the information available pertaining to your products and target group, but is that enough to make you a great salesperson? It certainly plays a big part, but it is not the entire story. So, what is it that truly makes a salesperson *exceptional*?

All great sales people have three things in common: **Excitement**, **Confidence**, and they **Believe in** the product or service they are providing. I just hate it when people say that you are either born a salesperson, or not. I agree that some people are naturally talented in sales, however, that does not mean that sales can't be taught. You are *already* a great salesperson and I can prove it to you.

Try to remember a time when you had a conversation amongst friends, and you were telling them about a great vacation you went on, a product you had recently bought and you just fell in love with, a hobby or passion of yours. Do you remember them wanting to find out more? I am sure they did; they might even have been sold on that vacation, hobby, or product, and asked you how they could acquire it themselves. Have you ever thought about why? The answer is simple and boils down to one word: **Excitement**.

You were happy, passionate, and excited about that one thing you **Believed in**, which is why you were able to communicate it in such a strong way. Well, I hate to break it to you, but this is sales.

You can sell anything to almost anyone, as long as you are able to transmit your excitement about it and show you strongly believe in it. Now, if you are selling kitchen appliances, you might argue that there is nothing exciting about an espresso machine; and I would disagree. There might not be anything exciting about an espresso machine to *You*, but I guarantee it can be and is exciting to numerous of the consumers buying it. So, what you need to do is discover what that exciting feature might be and start believing in the products or services you sell. However, if you are adamant about it and you don't believe in what you are offering, you can either change the product (assuming it is your company) or ask your manager to explain why he or she believes in that product, which will hopefully change your mind.

The third trait that all great salespeople have in common is **Confidence**. Think of any person who managed to sell you something you didn't need or want in the first place. I am sure they were as confident as it gets.

One aspect is to be confident in your products. As discussed in chapter 2, the more information you have pertaining to your products, the more confident in selling you will be. The other aspect is being confident in yourself; because people buy more, and easier from people who appear self-assured. This is because we are naturally drawn to people who exude confidence. So, what does a confident person look like?

1. They stand upright. They do not slouch.
2. They maintain an open body posture. They lean into conversations, not back (which makes others feel at ease talking to them).
3. They appear happy and smile. They do not look angry or irritated to be assisting you.
4. They speak up. They do not whisper.
5. They speak with authority. They approach every conversation free of doubt and rich with assurance, which is why their voice shows firmness.
6. They take their time to explain. They are not in a rush.
7. They listen. They do not care about pushing their own agenda. God (or nature, depending on your beliefs) gave you two ears and one mouth, so that you listen twice as much as you speak.
8. They take care of their appearance. Because looks MATTER. Don't get me wrong, this has nothing to do with beauty standards. What I mean is that they look "put-together", like they made an effort. If a person physically appears like they do not care about themselves (oily hair, chapped nail polish, wrinkled clothes, etc.), a customer's logical assumption is that this person does not care about their job either; or about their products and services for that matter. Whereas a more "put-together" person looks professional, leading customers to assume they are well acquainted with their job and their products or services.

Chapter 4.
Building Trust Based Relationships

The fourth step in selling any product or service effectively, is to build a trust-based relationship between you and your customer. This means getting the customer to like and trust you, which will undoubtedly increase your chances of selling. When you are able to connect with a client on a personal level, they will be one step closer to actually going through with the purchase.

A strong trust-based relationship depends on:

A. The knowledge you have regarding your products and company (Chapter 2)

B. The personal rapport you manage to form with your clients. This personal bond between you and the customer will strongly relate to the confidence you have in yourself and your products (Chapter 3).

Bonus tip: There are however two additional ways to get any person to like you, which are:

1. **Giving a compliment**
2. **Body Language Mirroring**

1. **Paying a compliment** is one of the easiest ways to get anyone to like you. However, in a sales setting this should be approached with caution, as you do not want to come across as...well, *creepy*. It is safer to compliment a client on an attribute they present, rather than their physical appearance. For example, complimenting a

customer on their sense of style, or the depth of knowledge they have regarding a topic instead of their looks.

2. **Body Language Mirroring.** You may have heard this amazing fact that only 7% of our communication is verbal and 93% is nonverbal. This is because we respond to body language more than we do to words. Having this knowledge means we can capitalize on it when we want a person, or a customer in our case, to like us. How? By using Mirroring. Body language Mirroring is the behavior in which one person unconsciously imitates the https://en.wikipedia.org/wiki/Gesturegesture, speech pattern, stance or attitude of another. We mirror each other's body language as a way of bonding, being accepted and creating rapport, but we are usually unaware we are doing it. It is actually quite simple, people like people who resemble themselves. So, how can you take advantage of this? Simply try to use the same voice tone as your customer or use the same hand gestures as them. If you see them nodding while talking to you, do the same. Put this to the test in any setting (family, friends, work, or even when meeting someone for the first time) and see the amazing results for yourself!

Bonus Tip: If you are working with clients that are not native to your mother-tongue, it would serve you to know a few words in their language in order to get them to like you. Allow me to share a short story. I once worked in a summer season location, that had tourists visiting mainly from 5 countries (Norway, Sweden, Holland, Germany, and Israel). So, I learned how to say "Amazing" and "Thank You" in all these languages. I used the word "amazing" in their language when demonstrating products to get them to laugh, and "thank you" when they left the store. It was my way of connecting with my customers and getting them to like and trust me easier. On one occasion, I was assisting a customer from Israel and said thank you in Hebrew when handing her the receipt of the purchase she had just made. She was almost in tears because, to her, it showed my respect for her and her country. This resulted in her coming back to the store every day (of her entire vacation) to make a purchase.

Chapter 5.
Asking the Right Questions (The 5 W's)

By now you know your audience, your product, you are confident, and you are starting to build a good rapport with your customer. So, your next step, which is in line with building a trust-based relationship, is to find the perfect product for them. Once you have a customer in front of you, you need to pose a series of questions regarding their needs in order to assist them in finding the ideal product or service that meets their demands. Some customers already know the exact product they are interested in purchasing and others do not; or they might have a general idea on what type of product they are after but are unsure which precise one to get. For example, they are looking to buy a couch for their living room, but do not know exactly which one to choose.

Whether a customer is buying a physical product or a service, your task is to adopt a line of questioning that will narrow down the options you will demonstrate to them. The easiest way to tackle this is to try phrasing your questions around the 5 W's, which are:

1. What
2. Who
3. Why
4. When
5. Where

Here are some examples incorporating the 5 W's in a question:

1. "**What** type of product are you looking to get?", "**What** is the most important feature you need this new machine to have?", "**What** occasion is this dress you are interested in meant for?"
2. "**Who** will be using this new computer the most in your household?", "Will there be anyone other than yourself, using this streaming service?", "To **whom** is this gift for? (family member, colleague, friend, acquaintance etc.)"
3. "**Why** are you interested in replacing the old TV set just now?", "May I ask **why** you are interested in this particular pair of shoes?", "**Why** do you prefer this specific color?"
4. "**When** would you expect to have the new security system installed?", " **When** will you be using this service?", "**When** do you plan on going on this vacation?", "By **when** do you need this product to be delivered to you?"
5. "**Where** do you picture yourself spending your retirement years?", "**Where** is the ideal location for your holidays?", "**Where** will you be wearing this shirt?"

The more information you are able to gather, the easier it will be for you to find the ideal product for your consumers. So, assuming that with your chosen line of questioning you were able to pin-point the perfect product for your customer, your next action should be to convince them to actually go through with the purchase. One way is to list the product benefits (How will the customer benefit from this product? What problem does this product solve for your customer?).

Another alternative is to get their senses involved. Get your customer to touch, hear, see, smell, and even taste your product. E.g. If a client is buying a car, get them to test drive it or to smell the leather seats. If you are selling clothes, urge the customer to try on the product so that they can see for themselves the amazing fit you described. If you are selling ice-cream, give the customer a sample tasting. The more senses involved in the buying process, the easier it will be for you to close the sale.

Chapter 6.
The Two Ways of Selling Any Product or Service

Whether you are selling a product, a service, or even yourself (at an interview for example), there are two ways you can go about it.

1. **Understanding the need of the customer.**
2. **Creating a need for the customer.**

1. Understanding the need of the customer, is discovering what the client is looking to purchase in order to solve a problem they are currently facing. For instance, a customer is in the market to buy a bigger car, as their family grew. Therefore, understanding the need of the customer in this example entails knowing **What** they need and **Why**. (depending on the situation and your chosen profession, you can use some or all of the 5 W's, as described in the previous chapter).

Bonus tip: As the customer is explaining to you their needs, it is essential for you to listen to the words and adjectives they are using when describing the product (comfortable, sexy, practical, etc). From this you can use synonyms or antonyms when you are presenting a product to them that matches their needs.

E.g. 1: Synonym = A customer says they need a dress for a first date and would like to look **sexy**. So, when you present her with different options, be sure to say how **seductive or sensual** the dress is.

E.g. 2: Antonym = A client says that he or she is interested in buying a new mattress as the one they already have is too hard. So, when you find the ideal mattress for them remember to stress how soft it is.

2. Creating a need for the customer is a bit more challenging, but just as effective. Simply put, it is when you manage to convince a customer they need something you have to offer, without them knowing they needed it in the first place (or at least, that was not the reason behind them visiting your store to begin with). An example would be a customer purchasing a t-shirt and you say "Now that the weather is changing, we also have some great jackets for you to try on". In this example, the customer came in to buy one thing, yet you were able to make them see how they might also need or benefit from another item you have to offer.

Being a great storyteller always facilitates in creating a need for a customer. That is being able to paint a picture (metaphorically speaking), a situation they can clearly imagine happening or a scenario they can picture finding themselves in. Some people are naturally born storytellers, others...not so much. Do not worry if you aren't a storyteller by nature, because there is a way to learn how to get better at it when it comes to sales. Just research any commercial related to your product. At the end of the day, all advertisements are short stories painting a picture for the consumer. This way you can use an existing narrative, transferring it to your product. Keep in mind that this does require a lot of practice, but practice make perfect!

Important note: Whichever of the two methods you decide to use, avoid lying to the customer at all costs. You might be able to make a sale this way, but you will have lost a repeat customer at the same time, and a possible good review (or an advocate for your brand). If, for example, you say to a customer they look great in the jeans you proposed, whereas in reality they can barely fit into them, this will eventually lead them to think you are only trying to make a sale and you are not really interested in helping them. Especially nowadays, people really appreciate honesty from salespeople and shopping assistants. I know that if I walked into a store that didn't have what I was looking for, I would truly appreciate it if the sales person said to me "Unfortunately, we do not have anything that matches your description, but there is a store down the road that does. We hope to be of service next time you visit our store!" Now, I would definitely return to that store, wouldn't you?

One final remark on the topic of lying to consumers. I often get asked whether or not you should lie to a customer if they are thrilled about a product, which in your opinion doesn't suit them. The reality is that the customer is (almost) NEVER right. There, I said it. You know it and I know it. However, it is completely irrelevant in this case. When it comes to your job and products, you probably know best. For example, you may know what type of trouser line suits each customer. Nevertheless, the customers usually do not care about you, or what you think, when it comes to the decision of them going through with the purchase. This is why it is important (in my experience) to let them have the final say. If they love the way a product looks on them, let them be happy with their decision and if you are not comfortable lying, simply deflect the question or answer in a more diplomatic manner. For example:

Customer: "This bikini is amazing! Doesn't it just look great on me? What do you think?"
You: Option 1. "It is really an amazing piece!"
      Option 2."All that matters is that you love it! You are the one who will be wearing it not me!"
      Option 3. "In my opinion people should always wear whatever makes them feel good!"

Chapter 7.
Understanding Emotional Triggers

Another excellent way to close any sale faster is to focus on the emotional triggers involved in the sale. As you may have heard before: "People buy emotions not products. They make a purchase based on emotion and justify it with logic." Therefore, it would benefit you if you managed to pinpoint the emotion lying beneath your client's purchase and use it when you are trying to close the sale. Some of the most well-known and powerful buying emotions include:

- Peer pressure (keeping up with the latest trends)
- Pride of possession
- Prestige and status
- Color and style
- Vanity
- Self-improvement
- Security
- Health & Fitness

Now that you are familiar with the triggers, you have two options. You can either discover which emotion led your customer to you, or evoke one of the listed emotions in your customers. Because learning how to evoke these emotions in your buyers will certainly enhance your earning potential. However, the exact phrases and words that you use will depend on your offering, your personality, your buyers, and market conditions. Study each of the selling emotions given above and develop a list of emotion-evoking questions you can ask your buyers.

Chapter 8.
The Five Questions You Should Be Asking Yourself

Whenever you are trying to close a sale and the customer doesn't appear to be sold on your offer, there are 5 questions that you need to ask yourself in order to be able to determine your course of action:

1. Does the customer **want** this product?
2. Does he or she want it **now**?
3. Is he or she willing to buy it at the given **price**?
4. Does he or she want to buy it **from you**?
5. Does he or she want to buy it from **your company**?

How many of these questions do you believe you can affect? In my entire career only two people have answered this question correctly. The answer is…ALL of them! Here is how:

1. **Does the customer want this product?** Were you sufficiently able to make them desire the product? It largely depends on you and your selling skills if the customer was convinced to buy the product.
2. **Does he or she want it now?** There is a way for you to affect whether the customer buys the product now, rather than them postponing the purchase. If you introduced a scarcity factor. For example, you mention that this is the last product left, or that a particular offer ends at the end of the day.

3. **Is he or she willing to buy it at the given price?** If a customer is not willing to buy a product at the given price there is always a reason behind it. Remember, people will spend more than they can afford if they fall in love with a product. So…did you make them fall in love with yours?

4. **Does he or she want to buy it from you?** If you managed to build a strong trust-based relationship with your customer (Chapter 4), the answer should be "Yes".

5. **Does he or she want to buy it from your company?** This can also depend on you, if for example, you were able to transmit effectively your knowledge on your company values or your company's quality standards (Chapter 2, point 10) .

Chapter 9.
Final Thoughts

In this book I have provided you with a number of different steps and ways to approach any sale. The only thing left is for you to take what you have learnt and put these methods to the test. I guarantee that all the methods mentioned work!

Try them out, practice, and do not give up on your first try! It may take a couple of tries to apply these methods and get them right in a way that will suit you. So, persist and find your own way to exploit these steps. Use your own language and line of questioning, because the way I word something might not feel comfortable to you.

Final Bonus tip: Try to make your **goal** to **Delight** the customer, and NOT to make a sale. Because if you only make your goal to close the sale, that will result in adding even more pressure on you. Once you are able to meet and exceed customers' expectations, the sale will follow organically.

Now get out there and starting closing all those sales!

Acknowledgments

I have to start by thanking my best friend, Maria Fioraki, who always urged me to write a book (even though this type of book was probably not what she had in mind!). So, thank you for always being there for me and never allowing me to give up! I would of course also like to thank my family, especially my parents, who I am forever indebted to for giving me the opportunities and experiences that have made me who I am and have shaped the way I think. A special thanks to my editor Jessica Fentiman, who made subtle changes effortlessly whilst keeping my voice!

Finally, I would like to thank all of you, my readers, to whom I can only hope I have provided some value to!